T0132070

Makeba's
New Adventure

Anthony D. Amaker

Print information available on the last page.

Rev. date: 02/01/2019

To order additional copies of this book, contact:
Xlibris
1-888-795-4274
www.Xlibris.com
Orders@Xlibris.com

Chapter I

On a sunny autumn day, Makeba woke up earlier than her usual. Her mother was busy in the kitchen preparing a special breakfast. It was not the ordinary cold cereal, for today was a very special day.

Makeba was only five years old, and her kindergarten party had just passed only a little over two months ago. It was June 19, of the year. She could still remember it very well, because her parents made such a big fuss about it.

Thinking back on the celebration, and the big party with all her friends. There was Michael, Malcolm, Taquan, Saquan, Dakim, amongst the young men. Keisha, Shanievah, Shakeyla, Latisha, and Jasmine amongst the young ladies. Everyone wore bright colors of green, orange, burgundy, white, black and gold.

Makeba was known as the young princess, and had a bright gold crown on her head. She wore a white gown with purple trimming. Purple was a royal color, and white indicating her purity. Her father was a brilliant gold and leather craftsman. He fashioned the crown with his own hands. He thought of Makeba as his special little princess, which he wanted to give her the world.

Everyone at the party brought hand made gifts, which were made with the aid of their parents. The adults all stayed in the guest room during most of the party. They all came in to check on the youth from time to time.

Makeba felt very grown up for her young years, but she knew that her parents had groomed her well. So as the guest of honor, she was to direct the games. She chose the name game, which was to describe your question to the audience of a famous black person in history. Whoever had the correct answer would gain ten points. The first in the group to gain 100 points would win a prize.

The first wonderful child to reach 100 points was Latisha, who named King Solomon, Queen Sheba, Ramses, Orsis, Horus, Isis, Booker T. Washington, Malcolm X, Elijah Muhammad and Marcus Garvey. There were others who in the party came close but not as quick as Latisha. The prize was a Vanilla flavor chew stick.

After the games, they watched a video tape of the Million Man March, and were very impressed by the young man their own age giving a speech. That's when Malcolm declared, "I'm going to be like him and speak for the people and to the people." To his surprise everyone at the party gave him a round of applause.

After the video was over the adults came out and the women headed to the kitchen to prepare the food. The men joined the children in the game room. The young children were asked prior to the feast to recite the seven principles or Nguzo Saba. These were deeply embedded into the children and Makeba's father wanted to see how much they knew. He wanted them to form a circle and he would place each of the children's names in a basket.

Then each of the men in the room would choose a name at random. Mr. Kenbolla was the first to reach in the basket and pulled out the first name. By surprise it was Jasmine, who was required to recite the first principle, which is "Umoja" meaning (Unity). After her reciting it first it was followed by the chorus of the young children collectively with the meaning. "To strive for and maintain unity in the family, community, nation and race." Mr. Akbar chose the second name Saquan, who immediately shouted, "Kujichagulia" meaning (Self-determination). It was followed by everyone. "To define ourselves, name ourselves, create for ourselves and speak for ourselves instead of being defined, named, created for and spoken for by others."

Mr. KaSun chose the third name, which was Malcolm who jumped to his feet. He shouted out "Ujima" meaning (Collective Work and Responsibility). Then everyone followed it with the definition "To build and maintain our community together, and make our sister's and brother's problems our problems and to solve them together."

Then Mr. Kareem chose the fourth name, which was Shakeyla who responded in a very gentle voice, "Ujamma" meaning (Cooperative Economic). Then everyone stated in unison, "To build and maintain our own stores, shops and other businesses and to profit from them together."

The next pick was Mr. Ali, who chose Dakim. He shouted really loud, "Nia" meaning (Purpose). Then everyone shouted "To make our collective vocation the building and developing of our community in order to restore our people to their traditional greatness."

Then Makeba's father pulled the sixth name from the basket, which was Michael. He spoke in a more timid voice "Kuumba" meaning (Creativity). Everyone followed behind him with the meaning, "To do always as much as we can, in the way we can, in order to leave our community more beautiful and beneficial than when we inherited it."

Since there was only one more principle left, everyone spoke at the same time. "Imani" meaning (Faith). "To believe with all our heart in our people, our parents, our teachers, our leaders, and the righteousness and victory of our struggle."
It was at the completion of the Nguzo Saba, that Ms. Ali came out from the kitchen. She informed everyone that the Karawei (feast) was prepared.

Everyone immediately went to wash up and then into the kitchen dining room area. Once they got there they were truly surprised. There was so much food that was African styled from the peanut fish stew to the pancake and the stir-fried okra. There was plenty of rich fruit such as mangos, pineapples, papayas, coconuts, bananas and plantains.

Yes, Makeba could easily remember this as if it were just yesterday. She couldn't wait for the next year to come for another party. Or for one of her close friends in the community to have a party.

Chapter II

The breakfast was extraordinary, which specially included eggs omelet with whiting fish, green peppers, tomatoes and onions inside, orange juice, wheat bread toast. Makeba being used to oatmeal was surprised by the hotcakes made with bran meal.

Her mother told her to get dressed in the bathroom but she wanted to finish cleaning her bedroom before they left. She came out of the bathroom in her light blue gown, which was trimmed with bright gold, red, white and black kente colors. She had patted herself down with talcum powder after she had brushed her teeth with baking soda. She put on her favorite oil of Sudanese Rose to make her smell fabulous.

She entered the dining room area of the kitchen with a question for her mother, "Mother, who made this wonderful table and breakfast?" Her mother responded, "Now honey, you know how much I love you and you're growing up now. We got a very busy day today and you're going to need a lot of energy."

Makeba sat at the table, and they began to eat their meal together. After the completion of the meal, Makeba's mother explained to her, "Honey you're going to start 1st grade and your father and I have picked a very special school for you." Makeba said: Mother I thought you and daddy were going to teach me all I needed to know at home. You told me the schools were designed to under educate black children." Her mother stated: "Baby, you're so smart and you have learned a lot at home. We found something special for you. Believe me, baby we've made all the proper decisions after we shopped around. We want to make sure that you learn your roots and historical background. If you don't like the school, then we'll do what we can to change that. Now, don't you worry yourself too much about this because we'll be out all day."

Now Makeba was a little upset because of the news she just heard. She never wanted to leave her mother's side. She always thought from speaking with her parents that she would be taught in the house. She asked her mother: "Mother, will I have all my old friends like Malcolm and Jasmine?" "Baby, you'll always have your close friends, but you'll make new ones too," her mother replied.

Makeba's face brightened up to a big smile. She asked her mother: "Mother where are we going that we'll be busy and out all day?" Her mother replied: "Honey, we'll have to get you some new clothes to wear because I'll have to find a job while you're in school."

Makeba sat in silence drinking the last of her orange juice. She had to really think hard on her mother's last statement. A job, work, but surely her mother had made all her beautiful clothes. She really couldn't think of a store with such high quality fashion as her mother's handiwork.

As she and her mother ventured from the house, Makeba was in for a very big surprised and a new adventure. For the shopping mall which they were going to was called "African Are Us."

Chapter III

African Are Us was a very big shopping mall and was very busy and crowded. As they pulled the car into the parking lot, they saw there were many people shopping early in the morning. It was a lovely sunny day and not very hot. Makeba could see rows and rows of stores in the Mall.

As they exited the car, Makeba held her mother's hand not wishing to get lost in such a big crowd of people. They walked along the walkway and passed a leather shop. They could see the craftsman at his work. He would have had many customers if it were later in the afternoon. They could see him stitching a pair of sandals on a lacing pony. When he noticed them watching through the window he smiled and waved at them. Both Makeba and her mother waved back at him and then they began to walk on to the dress shop a few doors down the walkway.

They stopped at the next small shop and entered. There was a tall beautiful black woman in a long silk green dress which ran down to her leather sandals. The sandals on her feet were gold trimmed and she wore a turban on her head of white silk. Makeba's mother stated: "We're going to purchase just a few rolls of silk and satin fabric because I still plan to make all your dresses after I start working, even if I just do it on a few weekends." Makeba started to look around at the different colors of bright silk and satin materials on the shop's wall racks as her mother and the woman spoke. They both moved around with the woman in the small shop.

To Makeba's surprise, the owner of the shop had a big aquarium in the shop. It contained hundreds of tropical fish in many different varieties. When her mother and the woman noticed her interest in the Aquarium, they approached her. The woman began to give Makeba the names of different fish in the Aquarium. Makeba smiled and the shop owner told her: "If you want to honey, you can feed them. It's just about their feeding time. However, you must always remember never to feed them too much." Makeba stated, "I would love to, if it is alright with my mother first." Makeba's mother responded, "It's alright baby, it's just another education for you to learn now. Someday you may have pets of your own and then you could apply the same learning techniques."

After she fed the tropical fish, then her mother purchased some beautiful bright colors silk and satin materials. There were purple, burgundy, teal, black, white, gold, brown, peach, green, blue and maroon silk and satin for her future clothing. Makeba could just imagine what her mother would do with all those bright colors. They soon left the store with a big bag on each arm.

It was about 10:30 a.m. and Mrs. Hakim figured they would go to one more shop before they would get a bite to eat. She had earlier thought about making lunch for herself and her daughter, however she decided to give her daughter Makeba a special treat for the day. Makeba's mother led her to a special Jewelry store, which made all kinds of handcrafted gold, silver and copper custom jewelry. A pearl and shark tooth necklace was what she and her husband decided to get their daughter.

Makeba looked around and saw a fantastic item. Makeba asked her mother, "What kind of jewelry is this?" Her mother responded, "I don't know honey but it looks like a pentacle of King Solomon." Little did she know how right she was.

The store clerk came from the back, so happy that the key of Solomon had caught someone's eye as it always did. "May I be of service to you, Madam?" the clerk asked. His voice coming from the back of the shop with a lot of bass. Mrs. Hakim quickly turned around with Makeba doing the same at the same time. Makeba was the first to reply with her young voice. A genuine question and amazing brilliance for a child of her age. "Sir, could you tell us what this over here is?" She pointed at the pentacle which was of a shinning gold behind a large glass case.

"Oh, that is a very special item, which was worn by the famous one and only King Solomon of the Israelites. It is the pentacle of Venus, which is said to attract "Love" and "Friendship" of all those who look upon the person who wears it. It also subjects that person to the will of the person who wears it," the clerk informed them.

With the explanation done, Mrs. Hakim stated, "That's very interesting but do you have a small pearl necklace of 16 inches with a genuine shark tooth attached?" The clerk replied, "Yes, we have some of those items in that category imported from the West Coast of Africa. I'll be very happy to show those to you if you and the young lady will step to the back."

They all moved to the rear of the store area and the clerk went through a back door. He reappeared moments later with a case, which he opened for Mrs. Hakim. In it was all the luxury to get to the business at hand and to Mrs. Hakim surprise. Everything was beautiful and really glamorous to her eyes. She looked the case over and saw the perfect one. She asked, "Now Makeba isn't this one just lovely?" When she did not get an answer to her question, she quickly turned around only to find Makeba standing and staring at the pentacle of King Solomon once again. She decided to let her fulfill her curiosity, and quickly and quietly made the purchase.

Upon leaving she nearly had to pull Makeba away from the pentacle. She made a mental note to tell her husband and maybe they'll get it for her next gift.

"Makeba, it's about 11:30 a.m. now it's time to eat. Are you hungry now?" Her mother asked.

That brought a smile to the young Makeba's face as they exited the jewelry store. They later arrived at a small African Shop, which was in the shape of a hut. Its appearance was excellent and Makeba was totally amazed at the sight.

Upon entering the restaurant, she noticed it had wooden tables and chairs. Behind the counter there were big cooking pots. There were bowls of fruits on each table. There was a bar to the far right, which displayed a sign that read closed until 5:30 p.m. The table where they sat, seated up to four persons. Upon sitting down, the waitress produced a menu and two glasses of fresh coconut milk with a little paper umbrella on top.

Illustrated by Grace Amaker

Mrs. Hakim said, "Honey, I'll order for the two of us okay, because I want you to try a dish, I sample here with your father." Makeba replied, "Okay mother."

She was still looking around from her chair at the beauty of the place. The place had windows and curtains in her favorite color Maroon. The carpet was a dark green color which she liked as well. It gave her a feeling of walking on grass. She saw that there were pictures all over the walls of all kinds of animals and birds. Some she knew and others she did not. It was all totally interesting to her young mind. Her mother noticed how big and bright her eyes were when she finally turned around in her seat once again.

Then as she was about to ask her another question, the waitress returned ready to take their order. "How are you and may I take your order now?" the waitress asked. "Oh, yes, we'll have number 4 on the menu and some more of this good coconut milk." Makeba's mother order. With that reply the waitress retreated and was gone.

Makeba asked her mother, "Mother, what is that picture of right over there?" As she pointed at the picture over her mother's right shoulder. As her mother looked, she noticed a beautiful Ostrich in flight with others on the plains of Africa. "Oh, baby, that's an Ostrich which is a big bird in Africa," her mother replied. As she was about to explain further, the waitress returned with their order. Makeba thought to herself that it looked like a lot of food. She wondered if she would be able to eat it all.

Illustrated by Grace Amaker

There was a salad bowl of melons, bananas, chunks of coconuts, mangos, raisins all covered with rich chocolate syrup. Then there was a plate full of fresh broil trout with lemon slices, baked potatoes covered with blue cream cheese sauce and fried plantain chips. Makeba had no more questions or words to say. She was very hungry from the traveling on the trip shopping with her mother. As she ate her food, she noticed a sweet cute smile on her mother's face.

Once they had completed their meal for the afternoon, then they continued on their shopping spree. They were finished by 3:00 p.m. and it had been a long fulfilling day of brand new adventure for Makeba. This was made possible by the kindness of her special friends and wonderful mother. Before they returned to the car to drive back home, she and her mother made one last stop. They entered the white castle shape shop and beheld that it was an Ice Cream Shop. Makeba's mother introduced her to another special treat and it was an extra special pleasure to her. "Makeba, I want you to try this new flavor ice cream before we go home" her mother stated. Makeba replied, "anything you say mother because today has been one of the best days I've had in a long time. Especially since my party, I can't remember having so much fun.

The counter was empty except for the two of them and Makeba's mother ordered a triple deluxe special cone. When Makeba laid her eyes on it, she was struck with amazement. It was an ice cream cone, shaped like a tree with three scoops of chocolate ice cream and there were big chunks of chocolate in it, as well as raisins and nuts. Makeba's mother explained that it all was imported from Africa and was very sweet. It needed no sugar to make it and was topped with sprinkles of coconut.

Illustrated by Grace Amaker

Well after they finished their last treat for the day, they returned to the parking lot each carrying two shopping bags. Since Makeba was the smallest of them, ordinarily her bags were small ones.

They reached their house at approximately 4:00 p.m. and Makeba's father was not home. She was a little saddened but knew she would have a story to tell her father once he came home from a long day of work. However, in the meantime, she realized she was very tired and wanted to take a nap before dinner.

She knew that when she did wake up, she would have a story of a new and great adventure at African Are Us to tell her father.

The End

About the Author

The author, Anthony D. Amaker, is an African American raised in the Williamsburg section of Brooklyn, New York. He grew up during the height of the civil rights era and has taken a special forum to the causes of the African American struggles.

He is now working on matters of self-esteem and development for Black children because they are truly our future. He has grown up with a strong mindset to foster ambition, goals and self worth in all the children that he encounters. He has been raised in a big family and believes highly in the process of family values. He hopes to spread a sense of joy with every book that's dedicated to the children of all ethnicity.

Printed in the United States
By Bookmasters